Silent Night
Arr. by Sharon Aaronson

The Alfred Duet Series

*Designed to bring you the best in duet music
by today's most talented composers.*

Silent Night

secondo

Franz Grüber
Arr. by Sharon Aaronson

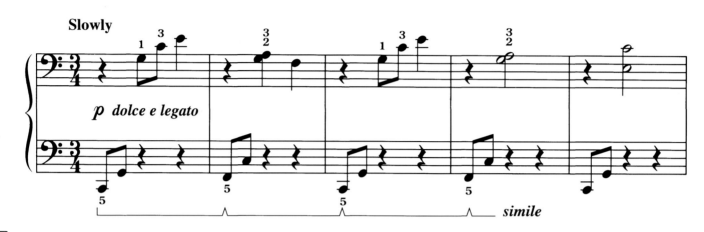

Silent Night

primo

Franz Grüber
Arr. by Sharon Aaronson

Slowly

Both hands one octave higher than written throughout

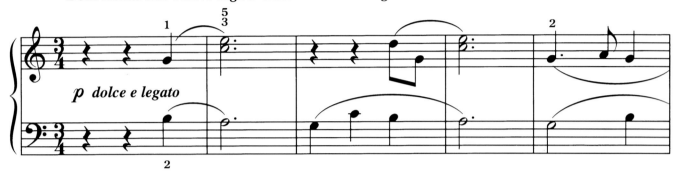

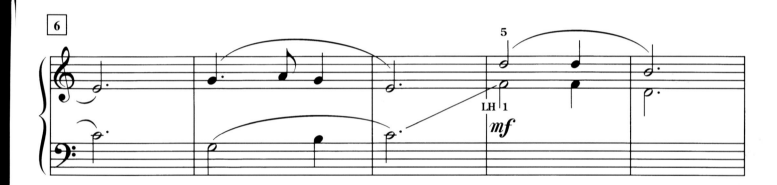

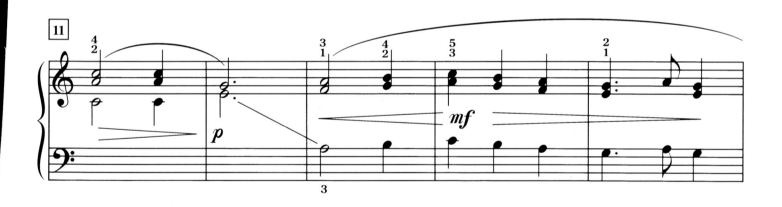

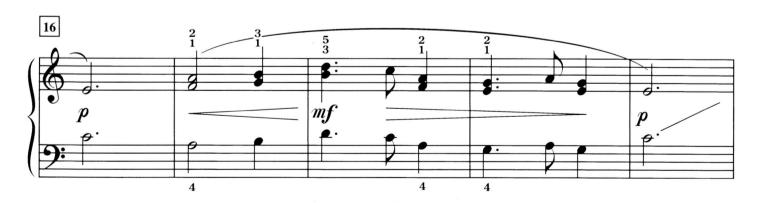

secondo

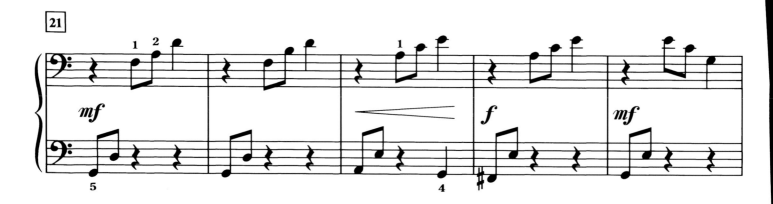

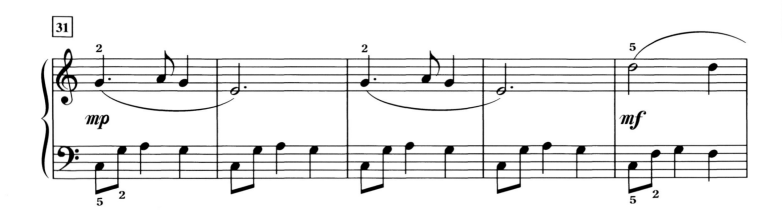

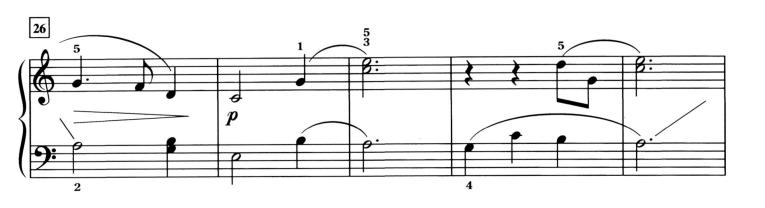

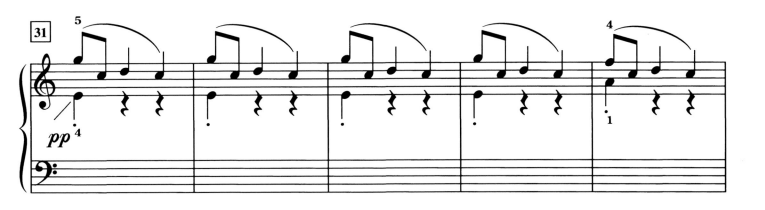

41

46

51

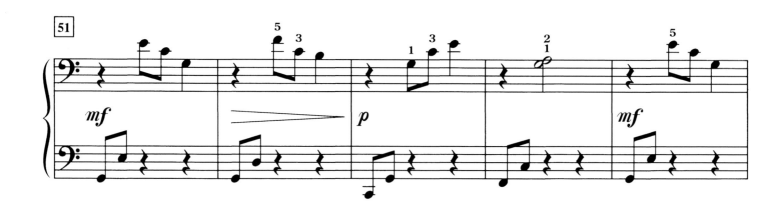

56

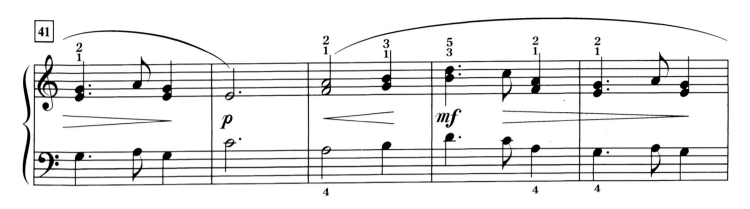

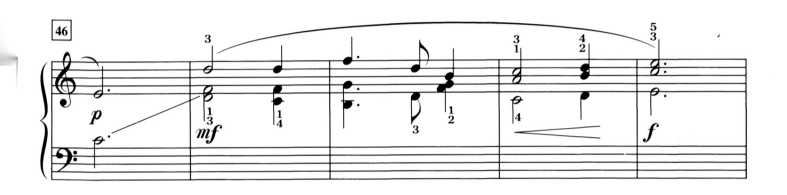

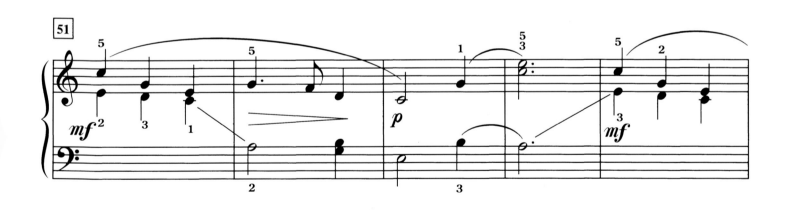

ISBN-10: 0-7390-0373-9
ISBN-13: 978-0-7390-0373-2

9 780739 003732

Alfred

alfred.com

18978 $4.99 in

W8-BIZ-101

0   38081 17657   4

ISBN 0-7390-0373-9